# Ryokan Life

I Talk You Talk Press

ISBN: 978-4-909733-73-3

www.italkyoutalk.com

info@italkyoutalk.com

# CONTENTS

I Talk You Talk Press

# 1. WHERE ARE THE GUESTS?

Yuka Nakata is a university student. She studies English. Her university is in Tokyo. Yuka is from a small town near Kyoto. In the town, her family own a ryokan. A ryokan is a Japanese-style hotel. Her family's ryokan is very old. Many tourists stay in the ryokan. Summer is very busy, so Yuka helps her family in the ryokan. Some tourists are from other countries, so Yuka talks to them in English. Yuka likes working at the ryokan. She can meet many people, and she can practice her English.

Now, it is August. Yuka is talking to two guests from Australia. The guests are a young man and a young woman. Their names are Ian and Kate.

"Good morning," says Yuka. "What are you going to do today?"

"We are going to go sightseeing in the town," says the man. "Yesterday, we went to Kyoto City, but there were many people. We want to go to a quiet place today. So, we are going to look around the town."

Yuka looks out of the window. "Now, it is very hot and sunny. But later, it will be very windy and rainy. Please take care."

Ian smiles. "It's OK. We will be fine! We will come back around five o'clock. Can we eat dinner around seven?"

"Sure, I will bring you dinner at seven. You can tell me about your day. Have a good time!" says Yuka.

That day, Yuka is very busy. She cleans the rooms, and she helps her mother and the chef prepare food. At around 3:00pm, she looks out of the window. The sky is grey. The wind is strong. It is raining.

*It is windy outside,* she thinks. *Are Ian and Kate OK?*

A group of guests comes to check in. Yuka is very busy. She doesn't have time to think about Ian and Kate. After the guests check in, Yuka goes to the kitchen. Her mother and the chef are preparing food.

"Do you need any help?" she asks.

"Yes, please," says the chef. "Can you make the miso soup? There are many guests today."

Yuka makes the soup. There are no windows in the kitchen, so she can't see the weather. After she makes the soup, she helps her mother make some vegetable dishes. Then, she goes out of the kitchen and into the lobby.

She looks out of the window. "Oh no! There is a storm! It is like a typhoon!" The rain and wind are very strong. The sky is dark. She looks at the clock. It is 5:30pm.

She goes to the front desk. She asks the man on the front desk, "Did the Australian man and woman come back?"

"No, not yet," says the man.

"I am worried," says Yuka. "The weather is very bad."

"Maybe they will come back soon," says the man. "The museum closes at five thirty. Maybe they went to the museum."

Yuka helps her mother take food to the guests' rooms. She is very busy. When she stops, she looks at the time. It is 7:30pm. She goes to Ian and Kate's room and knocks on the door. There is no answer. She knocks again.

*They are not back yet. Something is wrong. Where did they go today?* she thinks.

Yuka goes into the room. She looks at the table. There are some tourist pamphlets on the table. She picks up one of the pamphlets.

*Oh no! The temple on the mountain!* she thinks. *They went to the big temple on the mountain! The weather is very bad. The mountain is dangerous!*

Yuka runs out of the room and goes to her father's office.

"Two guests went to the temple on the mountain," she says. "They are not back yet."

"They went to the mountain? In this weather?" Her father is very shocked.

"I'm going to drive to the mountain and look for them," says Yuka.

"It is too dangerous," says her father.

"It's OK," says Yuka. "I will drive the big truck. I will be fine."

Her father looks at her. "We are very busy. So I can't go with you.

Please be careful. And call me if you need help."

"OK," says Yuka. She goes to her bedroom and takes off her kimono. She puts on her jeans and a T-shirt. She goes downstairs and puts her shoes on. She goes out of the ryokan and runs to the car park. The rain is very heavy. She gets in the truck and drives to the mountain.

There is a small road on the mountain. The road goes to the temple.

*I think the man and woman are on this road. I will drive up to the temple. Maybe I will see them.*

There are trees on both sides of the road. It is very dark. Yuka drives carefully and looks around. Near the temple, she sees a person. The person runs in front of the truck. Yuka stops. It is Kate!

Kate gets in the truck. She is very wet.

"Are you OK? What happened?" asks Yuka.

"I'm OK, but Ian is not OK. It was very dark, and he fell over. His foot is very bad. I think it is broken. He can't walk. I wanted to call the ryokan, but I can't use my phone on the mountain. There is no signal. I'm so happy to see you. Please help us."

"OK, where is Ian?" asks Yuka.

"He is about a hundred metres up the road," says Kate.

Yuka drives slowly. "Why didn't you come down the mountain earlier?" she asks.

"The weather was bad. We thought, 'If we wait, the rain will stop.' So we waited. But the rain didn't stop. So, we started walking. Then Ian fell over. Please stop here."

Yuka stops the truck, and the two women get out.

"Ian!" says Kate. "Are you here?"

"Yes!" says Ian.

They walk to Ian. "Yuka!" says Ian. He is very surprised. "I'm so happy to see you!"

"I'm going to help you," says Yuka. "I'm going to take you to the hospital."

Kate and Yuka help Ian to walk to the truck. They all get in the truck.

"I have a problem," says Yuka. "The road is small. I can't turn the truck around. I will drive to the temple car park and turn around there."

Yuka drives to the temple car park and turns around. Then, she drives slowly down the mountain.

"You are a good driver, Yuka," says Kate. "The road is small and there are many trees. It is very dark, and it is raining."

Yuka drives to the hospital in the town. A doctor looks at Ian's foot. It is broken. He has to stay in hospital for a few days. Yuka takes Kate back to the ryokan. Kate has a bath and then Yuka takes her some food.

"Thank you, Yuka. I am so hungry!" says Kate. "And thank you for helping us."

"You're welcome," says Yuka. "At this ryokan, we do our best to help our guests!"

A week later, Ian comes out of hospital, and Ian and Kate go back to Australia.

Three weeks later, a package arrives at the ryokan. The package is for Yuka. She opens it. Inside, there is a handbag and some candy. There is also a note. Yuka reads the note.

*---Thank you so much for helping us. We will never forget you, from Ian and Kate.---*

Yuka smiles. The bag is beautiful, and the candy is delicious.

*I like working here,* she thinks. *The job is hard, but it is always interesting!*

## 2. THE WOMAN IN THE BIG COAT

Yuka looks at the woman at the front desk. The woman is checking in. She is alone. She is around 60 years old. But something is strange. It is August, and it is 36 degrees every day. It is very hot. But the woman is wearing a big winter coat.

*Why is she wearing a big winter coat?* thinks Yuka.

Later, Yuka takes dinner to the woman's room.

"Excuse me," she says. "I brought your dinner."

"Oh, thank you," says the woman.

Yuka is very surprised. The woman is sitting at the table. And she is wearing the big winter coat!

"Are you cold?" asks Yuka. "Is the air-conditioner too strong for you?"

"No, no," says the woman smiling. "It is fine. Everything is fine. Thank you."

The woman looks at the food on the table. "But, could I have a sausage please?"

"A sausage?" asks Yuka.

"Yes, a big sausage," says the woman.

"Er….yes, I think I can find a sausage for you," says Yuka.

She walks out of the room and goes down to the kitchen.

She says to her mother, "The woman in the big coat wants a sausage."

"A sausage?" Yuka's mother is surprised. "Why does she want a sausage?"

"I don't know. But she wants a big sausage."

"A big sausage?" asks Yuka's mother. She looks at the chef. "Do we have big sausages?"

The chef looks in the refrigerator. "We have small sausages. We can give the guest about three or four small sausages."

"OK, that's fine," says Yuka. The chef cooks the sausages and puts them on a plate. Yuka takes the plate to the woman's room.

The woman is eating. She is still wearing her big coat.

"I'm sorry, we don't have big sausages, so I brought four small sausages," says Yuka.

The woman smiles. "That is fine," she says. "Thank you. Can you bring me sausages every morning for breakfast, and every evening for dinner?"

"Er, sure," says Yuka. "We can do that."

Yuka goes out of the room.

*Maybe the woman likes sausages,* she thinks.

The woman is staying at the ryokan for four nights. Every morning and every evening, Yuka takes four sausages to the woman's room. The woman is always wearing the big coat. In the afternoons, the woman goes out. She wears her big coat.

*It is so hot outside!* thinks Yuka. *Where does she go?*

All the staff in the ryokan are talking about the woman. "Why is she wearing a big coat? Where does she go in the afternoons? Why does she eat so many sausages?"

It is the woman's last day at the ryokan. Yuka has an idea.

*When the woman goes out, I will follow her,* she thinks.

At 1:00pm, the woman goes out of the ryokan. A few seconds later, Yuka also goes out of the ryokan. The woman walks to the park in the centre of the town. Yuka also walks to the park. In the park, the woman takes something out of her coat, and puts it on the ground.

Yuka is shocked. It is a small dog! Then, the woman takes her coat off. She carries her coat and walks with her dog. Then, the dog looks behind, and runs to Yuka.

*Oh no! The dog is coming to me! The woman will see me!* thinks Yuka.

The woman turns around. "Ami-chan, come here!" she says to the dog. Then, she sees Yuka.

Yuka smiles.

"Oh no!" says the woman. "Now you know my secret! I'm so sorry. We can't take pets to your ryokan, but…" The woman looks sad.

"Let's sit on this bench," says Yuka. They sit on a bench. "Are you

OK?" asks Yuka.

"Yes, I'm OK, but I'm very sorry," says the woman.

The dog jumps up and sits between Yuka and the woman.

"Why did you bring your dog?" asks Yuka.

"Every year, for thirty years, my husband and I went to a ryokan in summer. He died in spring this year. I was very sad and lonely, so my daughter bought me a dog. It is summer. I wanted to go to a ryokan. But I didn't want to go alone. So, I brought Ami-chan."

"Are the sausages for Ami-chan?" asks Yuka.

"Yes, they are," says the woman. She looks at Yuka. "Are you going to tell your mother and father?" she asks. "I did a bad thing. I will have a lot of trouble."

Yuka thinks about it. The woman's husband died. She was sad and lonely. She wanted to go to a ryokan, but she wanted to take her dog too. *It is a sad story,* she thinks.

"When are you going home?" asks Yuka.

"Tomorrow morning," says the woman.

"It's OK. I won't tell my mother and father. It's our secret."

The woman smiles. "Thank you so much. You are a very kind young lady."

The woman puts the dog under her coat and goes back to the ryokan. Yuka goes to the meat shop and buys two big sausages.

Later, at dinner time. Yuka takes dinner to the woman. The woman is sitting at the table. She is wearing her big coat.

"I brought your dinner," she says. "And I brought two big sausages for Ami-chan. I hope she likes them!"

The woman smiles. "You are so kind. Ami-chan will be very happy." The woman puts the dog on the floor. Yuka gives the sausages to the dog. The dog eats the sausages very quickly.

The next morning, the woman checks out. "Goodbye, and thank you for staying with us," says Yuka's mother. Yuka and her mother watch the woman leave the ryokan.

"So why is she wearing that coat?" asks her mother.

"I don't know," says Yuka. "It is a mystery!"

## 3. THE PASSPORT

It is 6:00am. Two guests from Spain, Diego and Jose, are checking out.

"Thank you very much. We had a wonderful time," says Jose. "You and all the staff here are very nice."

"Thank you, too," says Yuka. "Thank you for choosing our ryokan. What time is your flight?"

"It is at eleven thirty," says Diego.

"The train from here to Kyoto takes thirty minutes. Then the train from Kyoto to Kansai Airport takes seventy-five minutes. What time do you have to check in?"

"Around eight thirty," says Diego. "We will be fine."

"Have a good trip!" says Yuka. She watches the two men walk out of the ryokan. She closes the door, and goes to the kitchen to prepare breakfast for the guests.

At 8:15am, she goes to clean Diego and Jose's room. She takes the sheets off the futons and cleans the table.

"Oh no!" Yuka looks under the table. There is a passport. She opens it. It is Diego's passport.

*Diego can't travel without a passport!* she thinks. *What can I do?*

She runs out of the room with the passport and finds her mother.

"Diego's passport is here!" she says. "What should we do?"

"Oh no!" says her mother. "What time is their flight?"

"Eleven thirty," says Yuka. "I have to give this passport to Diego. If I drive to the airport, I can give him the passport."

"It will take about two hours to drive to the airport," says her mother. "If you leave now, you will arrive at the airport at around ten thirty."

"But they have to check in around eight thirty. Maybe ten thirty is too late. But, I have to do something. OK, I'm going to the airport!" says Yuka. She goes up to her room to change her clothes. She takes the car keys from the front desk, puts her shoes on and runs to the car park.

*I will drive quickly,* she thinks. She gets in the car, and starts to drive. There are not many cars on the road. When she leaves the town, she takes the highway. She drives very fast. She listens to the radio. Soon, she is at Kansai Airport.

She finds a parking space and runs into the airport. She goes up to the departure lounge and looks around.

*There are so many people!* she thinks. *How can I find Diego and Jose?* She runs through the airport. She looks at all the people sitting on chairs. Then, she sees the two men.

Diego's suitcase is open. His clothes and other items are on the floor. Jose is looking in Diego's bag. The two men look very worried.

"Diego! Jose!" shouts Yuka.

Diego and Jose look up.

"Yuka!" says Diego.

"I have your passport!" says Yuka. "It was under the table in your room!"

Diego and Jose stand up. They hug Yuka.

"Oh Yuka, you are wonderful!" says Diego.

"Quick! You have to check in!" says Yuka. She helps the men pack Diego's suitcase and bag. The men hug her again, and then go to the check-in counter.

*Is it too late to check in?* thinks Yuka. She is worried. She watches the men.

Then, Diego and Jose wave to her.

"It's OK!" shouts Diego. "Thank you so much! We are going to give you a five star review on Trip Advisor!"

Yuka laughs. "Have a great flight!"

# 4. SHADOWS ON THE SCREENS

"Aaahhh!! Help! Someone help me!"

Yuka wakes up. She looks at the time. It is 3:30am.

"Help! Help!"

*What is that?* she thinks. *It is a guest. The guest needs help.*

Yuka gets up from her futon and runs out of her bedroom.

"Help! Help!"

*It is the guest in the room on the first floor,* she thinks. *The young Canadian woman. Is she sick?*

Yuka knocks on the door. "Vicky, are you OK?" she asks.

"Yuka! Please help me!" shouts Vicky.

"Can I come in?" asks Yuka.

"Yes!" says Vicky.

Yuka goes into Vicky's room. She switches the light on. Vicky is sitting in her futon. She is crying.

"What happened?" asks Yuka.

"There is a ghost in this room!" says Vicky.

"A ghost? No. This ryokan is old, but we don't have a ghost," says Yuka.

"But I saw the ghost of a man! A big man! I saw the shadow on the screen!"

There are Japanese paper screens covering the windows of the room.

"A shadow? That's strange," says Yuka.

"It's a ghost!" says Vicky.

Yuka slides the screen and opens the window. She can see the garden and a wall. There is a light on the other side of the wall.

*This is at the back of the ryokan,* she thinks. *No people will come into the garden at this time. What did Vicky see?*

"I can't stay in this room," says Vicky. "Can I change rooms?"

"I'm sorry, there are no free rooms tonight. You can change rooms tomorrow night," says Yuka.

"But I can't sleep here tonight! I am too scared! I saw a ghost!" says Vicky.

Yuka thinks. Then she says, "I will sleep in this room with you."

Vicky looks at Yuka. "Really? Oh, thank you Yuka. I will feel safe if you are here."

Yuka takes a futon out of the closet and puts it on the floor.

"Don't worry. Let's try to sleep," says Yuka. "Good night."

"Good night," says Vicky.

Soon, the two women are asleep.

The next morning, some guests check out, and there is a room free on the second floor.

"Vicky, you can change rooms," says Yuka. "We will help you take your suitcase to the new room."

"Thank you so much," says Vicky. "That room on the first floor is scary!"

The staff take Vicky's suitcase to the new room.

At 3:00pm, more guests check in. A man and a woman will stay in the room on the first floor.

Yuka goes to the room to give the man and the woman some tea. She knocks on the door and goes into the room. The man and the woman are sitting next to the window.

"This is a beautiful room," says the woman. "The garden is wonderful."

"Thank you," says Yuka. She gives them some tea.

*I hope they don't see anything strange!* she thinks.

The next morning, the man and the woman get up early. Yuka is preparing breakfast in the kitchen.

"Yuka, two guests would like to speak to you," says a staff member.

Yuka goes out of the kitchen. She sees the man and the woman. They look very tired.

"Good morning. Is everything OK?" she asks.

"No," says the man.

"No! There is a ghost in the room!" says the woman.

*Oh no,* thinks Yuka.

"A ghost? We don't have a ghost here," says Yuka.

"There was a noise around three thirty this morning," says the man. When we opened our eyes, we saw a big shadow on the paper screens."

"The shadow was big! It was a man!" says the woman.

"It wasn't a person, because outside the window there is only a garden. No one walks in the garden at three thirty am," says the man.

"Can we change rooms?" asks the woman. "I can't stay in that room tonight."

"Of course," says Yuka. "Our staff will take your suitcases to a different room."

Yuka goes back into the kitchen. She tells her mother about Vicky, and the man and the woman.

"This is very strange," says her mother.

"I have an idea," says Yuka. "I will sleep in the room tonight. I will wake up at three am and wait for the ghost."

"Good idea!" says her mother. "But I'm sure there is no ghost!"

At 11:00pm, Yuka puts a futon on the floor of the room. She gets into the futon. She reads a book for thirty minutes, and then she sets the alarm on her phone for 3:00am. She switches the light off and goes to sleep.

At 3:00am, the alarm on her phone rings. She switches the alarm off and waits. The room is not very dark. There is a street light on the other side of the wall, so she can see shadows. She waits. At 3:25am, she hears a noise.

*What is that?* she thinks. There is a noise outside in the garden.

Then, she sees a shadow on the screen. The shadow is big, and it looks like a man.

Yuka gets up quickly and runs to the window. She opens the screen and opens the window.

There is a man.

"Hey!" she shouts. "What are you doing?"

The man looks at her. "I'm sorry," he says quietly.

Yuka looks at him. "Nakamura san?" she says.

"Yes, it's me. Nakamura," says the man.

Mr Nakamura lives on the other side of the ryokan.

"Why are you in our garden at this time?" asks Yuka.

"I'm sorry. I changed my job. Now, I work in a factory. I start work at five pm and I finish at two thirty am. I walk home. I walk through your garden because it is quicker than the road."

"I see," says Yuka. "You are scaring our guests. Please don't walk through our garden."

"I'm very sorry. I won't do it again," says Mr Nakamura.

Yuka closes the window and the paper screen. She goes back to her futon and goes to sleep. The next morning, she sees her mother.

"Did you see the ghost?" asks her mother.

Yuka tells her mother about Mr Nakamura. Her mother smiles.

"So we have no ghost!" she says.

"No," says Yuka. "Mr Nakamura did a bad thing, but it is better than a ghost!"

## 5. THE DINNER BEFORE THE WEDDING

The ryokan has a big room for parties. This evening, there is a big party. A woman from the town will get married to a man from Kyoto. Her family and the man's family will have a party at Yuka's ryokan. There will be twenty people at the party. They will sit on cushions on the floor and eat many delicious dishes at low tables. The woman's family will sit on one side, and the man's family will sit on the other side.

Yuka, her mother and father, and all the staff are very busy. They arrange the room and cook a lot. The guests start arriving at 5:30pm. The party will start at 6:00pm.

Yuka goes out to the front door area and greets the guests. She takes them to the party room. She knows the woman's family. They live in the town. They smile when they see Yuka.

"How's university?" asks the woman's mother.

"It's good. I'm studying English. Next year, I will go to the UK for six months."

"That's great!" says the woman's mother. "Next year, maybe I will be a grandmother!"

Yuka smiles and takes the family to the party room.

Next, the man's family arrives. They are from Kyoto, so Yuka doesn't know them. She takes them to the party room.

The guests sit down at the tables. They are smiling and talking. But one guest is not smiling or talking. One guest looks very shocked. The guest is a woman from the man's family.

Yuka looks at her. *Is she OK? Is she sick?*

Yuka and her mother take drinks and food to the guests. Some people make speeches. Then, everyone drinks.

Everyone is talking loudly. They are having a good time. Yuka takes more food to the guests. She looks at the woman.

*She is not eating,* she thinks. *Why not?*

Yuka goes to the woman. She says very quietly, "Are you OK? Are you sick?"

The woman looks at Yuka. "I'm not sick. But.... Can I go to another room and rest?"

"Of course," says Yuka. The woman stands up. She goes out of the room with Yuka. They go to the office. "You can rest here," says Yuka.

"Thank you," says the woman. She sits down on a chair. "I had a big shock."

"Is there a problem with the food?" asks Yuka.

"No, no," says the woman. "There is a man. His name is Hiroshi Yamamoto."

"Oh, I know Mr Yamamoto!" says Yuka. "He has a company in the town. It is a printing company. When his father died, he became the president of the company."

The woman looks sad.

"Did Mr Yamamoto do something bad to you?" asks Yuka.

"No. He is a very nice man," says the woman.

"I think so too," says Yuka. "His family is very nice too."

"Today is the first time for me to see his family," says the woman. She looks at Yuka.

"When I was at university, he was my boyfriend," she says.

"Oh really?" says Yuka. She is surprised.

"Yes. I loved him. I wanted to marry him. But he didn't want to get married. He wanted to travel around the world. So, after university, he started travelling."

"Yes," says Yuka. "He has been to many countries. Did you see him when he came back?"

"No," says the woman. "I had a new boyfriend and a job. I was very busy. But, I still love him." She looks at Yuka. "Is he married?"

"No," says Yuka. "He is single."

"I am single too," says the woman.

"Do you want to talk to him?" asks Yuka.

"It is very difficult to talk to him. There are so many people here this evening," says the woman.

"Wait a minute," says Yuka. She goes out of the office and into the party room. Everyone is drinking, eating and talking. Yuka goes to Mr Yamamoto.

"Yamamoto san, I want to talk to you. Can you come with me, please?"

Mr Yamamoto looks surprised. "Yes, of course. But, is there a problem?"

"No, there is no problem," says Yuka.

Yuka and Mr Yamamoto go out of the room. "Someone would like to see you," says Yuka. They go into the office.

The woman looks up. "Hiroshi!" she says.

Mr Yamamoto looks at her. "I'm sorry, I don't know you," he says.

"It's me! Kyoko!" says the woman.

"Kyoko! I'm sorry! You look different! Your hair, your clothes, everything is different!"

Hiroshi sits down next to Kyoko.

"How are you?" he asks.

"I'm OK," says Kyoko. "But when I saw you, I had a shock."

"I'll bring you some tea," says Yuka.

She goes to the kitchen and makes some tea. Then she takes it to the office. Kyoko and Hiroshi are talking a lot.

The party finishes at 8:00pm. The guests go home. Yuka goes to the office. Kyoko and Hiroshi are still talking. They exchange phone numbers. When they see Yuka, they stand up.

"I'm sorry," says Hiroshi. "It is late."

"It's no problem," says Yuka.

Hiroshi and Kyoko go out of the office, and Yuka takes them to the front door. They say goodbye.

*They look like a nice couple,* thinks Yuka. She goes to the party room and helps her mother.

In September, Yuka goes back to Tokyo and back to university. A few months later, she gets a message from her mother.

*---We have some good news in the town. Hiroshi Yamamoto will get married! He met his girlfriend at our ryokan! Her name is Kyoko! They will have a wedding party here in March. They want to invite you to the wedding!---*

Yuka smiles. *I love happy endings,* she thinks.

# THANK YOU

Thank you for reading Ryokan Life. We hope you enjoyed the stories. (Word count: 4,816)

If you would like to read more graded readers, please visit our website http://www.italkyoutalk.com

Other Level 1 graded readers include
A Business Trip to New York
Adventure on the Mountain
A Homestay in Auckland
A Trip to London
Dear Ellen
Emily's Bag
Haruna's Story Part 1
Haruna's Story Part 2
Haruna's Story Part 3
Jimmy Luther
Ken's Story Part 1
Ken's Story Part 2
Life is Surprising!
Saori and the Storm
Strange Stories
The Christmas Present
The Old Hospital
Wei's Part Time Job

## We Met Online

# ABOUT THE AUTHOR

I Talk You Talk Press is an award-winning Japan-based publisher of language textbooks, graded readers and language learning/teaching resources. We won the Language Learner Literature Award in 2019 and 2020.

Our team is made up of highly experienced language teachers and translators, who have all studied at least one additional language to an advanced level.

This experience enables us to design our materials from the perspective of both the teacher and the learner. We consult with both teachers and language learners when designing our textbooks and graded readers, and test our materials extensively in the classroom before publication.

We are a fast-growing press, and currently publish graded readers for learners of English. We publish new graded readers monthly.

www.ingramcontent.com/pod-product-compliance
Lightning Source LLC
LaVergne TN
LVHW042241190726
843491LV00003BA/1184

* 9 7 8 4 9 0 9 7 3 3 7 3 3 *